Simple Machine Science

Screws

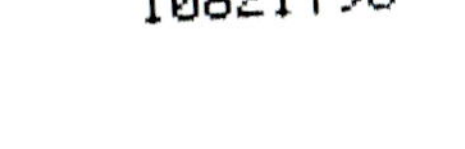

By Jerry Miller

Please visit our website, www.garethstevens.com. For a free color catalog of all our high-quality books, call toll free 1-800-542-2595 or fax 1-877-542-2596.

Library of Congress Cataloging-in-Publication Data

Miller, Jerry, 1951-
Screws / Jerry Miller.
p. cm. — (Simple machine science)
Includes index.
ISBN 978-1-4339-8147-0 (pbk.)
ISBN 978-1-4339-8148-7 (6-pack)
ISBN 978-1-4339-8146-3 (library binding)
1. Screws—Juvenile literature. I. Title.
TJ1338.M48 2013
621.8'82—dc23

2012021890

Published in 2013 by
Gareth Stevens Publishing
111 East 14th Street, Suite 349
New York, NY 10003

Designer: Katelyn E. Reynolds
Editor: Greg Roza

Photo credits: Cover, p. 1 Georgi Roshkov/Shutterstock.com; pp. 3–24 (background graphics) mike.irwin/Shutterstock.com; pp. 5, 7, 17 iStockphoto/Thinkstock.com; pp. 9, 11 Martin Poole/ Digital Vision/Thinkstock.com; p. 13 v.s.anandhakrishna/Shutterstock.com; p. 15 PhotoLink/ Photodisc/Getty Images; p. 19 Universal Images Group via Getty Images; p. 21 RTimages/ Shutterstock.com.

Printed in the United States of America

CPSIA compliance information: Batch #CW13GS: For further information contact Gareth Stevens, New York, New York at 1-800-542-2595.

Contents

Lots of Screws 4
What Is an Inclined Plane? 6
Around and Around 8
Keep It Together 10
Nuts and Bolts 12
Tool Time 14
Drills and Holes 16
Moving Water 18
Screws in the Kitchen 20
Glossary 22
For More Information 23
Index 24

Boldface words appear in the glossary.

Lots of Screws

A screw is a simple machine. You can find screws almost everywhere you go. They're used to hold wood together. Many tools use them, too. Some can even be used to move water. Let's find out how!

What Is an Inclined Plane?

An **inclined** plane is a flat **surface** that makes it easier to move something from one **height** to another. A ramp is an inclined plane. A screw is an inclined plane wrapped around a rod. The **thread** is a ramp.

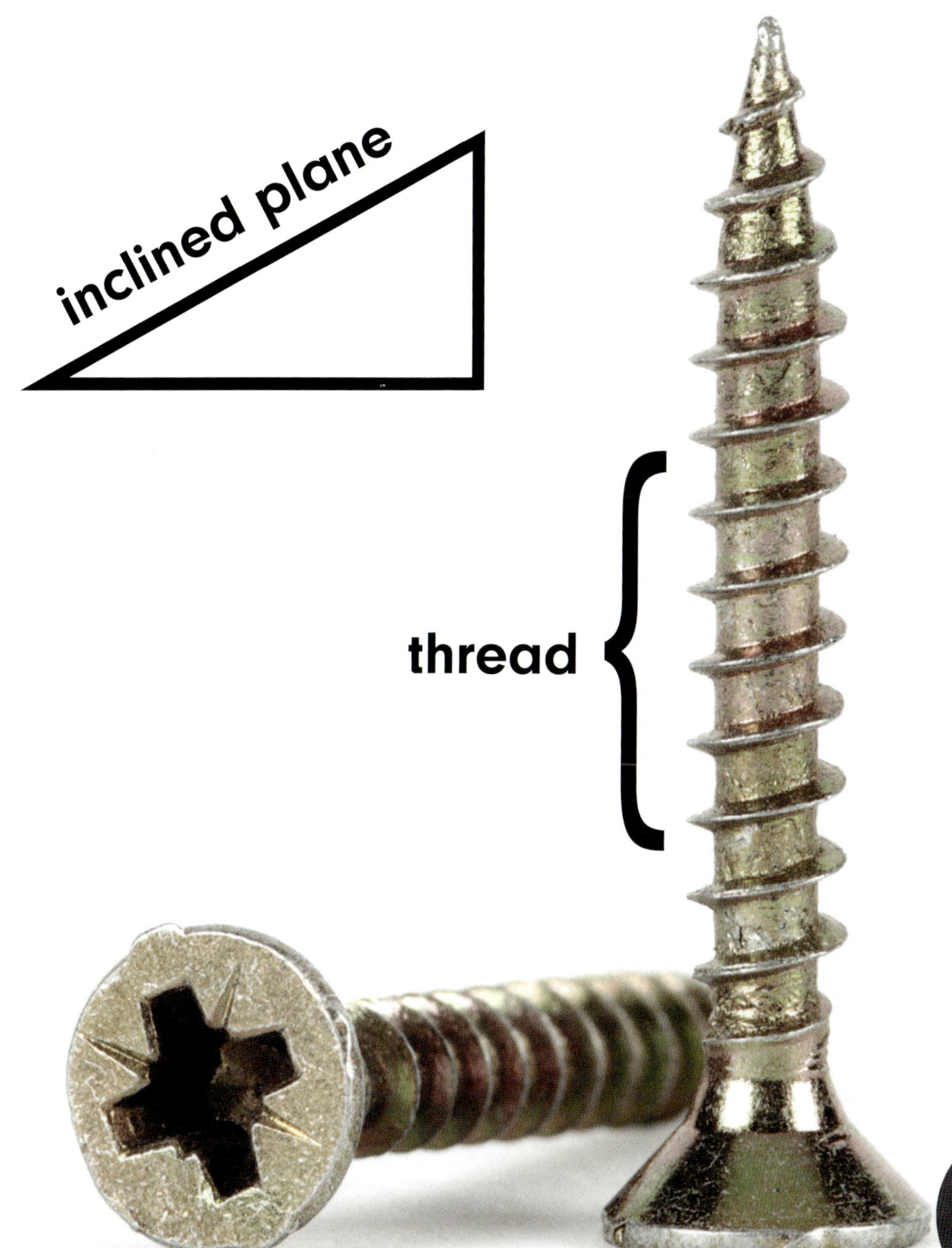
inclined plane
thread

Around and Around

Screws change a turning movement to an up-and-down movement. That's what happens when you use a screwdriver to turn a screw. When the screw turns, the thread grabs the wood and pulls the screw down into it.

Keep It Together

Screws are used to hold things tightly together. They're often used to fasten boards together. The screw goes through one board and then into the other. When the screw is all the way in, the two boards won't come apart.

11

Nuts and Bolts

A bolt has a thread around it. A nut has a thread inside of it. They fit together. When you turn the nut, it moves up or down the bolt. Nuts and bolts are used to hold parts together and keep them from moving.

bolt
nut

Tool Time

Many tools use screws. A clamp holds two things tightly together so you can work on them. Some people use clamps when gluing pieces of wood together. Some jacks use screws to lift heavy objects, such as cars.

15

Drills and Holes

Drills use turning movement to make holes in wood. Drills have parts called drill bits. A drill bit is threaded like a screw. As the drill bit spins, the thread cuts the wood and moves it out of the way.

Moving Water

Screws can also be used to move water to higher places! When the end of the screw that's underwater turns, the thread scoops up water. The turning movement carries water to the top of the screw.

Screws in the Kitchen

Jar lids are held on by screws—one on the jar and one inside the lid. You turn the lid to open the jar. You turn the lid the other way to close the jar. Screws keep your peanut butter fresh!

Screws in Our World

wood screw	nut and bolt	drill bit	clamp	car jack	peanut butter jar	water screw

Glossary

height: how tall or high something is

inclined: with one end higher than the other

surface: a hard, flat area

thread: the part on a screw that sticks out and winds around it

For More Information

Books

Bodden, Valerie. *Screws*. Mankato, MN: Creative Education, 2011.

Gosman, Gillian. *Screws in Action*. New York, NY: PowerKids Press, 2011.

Smith, Siân. *Screws, Nuts, and Bolts*. Chicago, IL: Heinemann Library, 2013.

Websites

Screws
www.historyforkids.org/scienceforkids/physics/machines/screw.htm
Read more about screws and discover more examples.

Simple Machines
www.edheads.org/activities/simple-machines/
Learn about simple machines through this fun interactive website.

Publisher's note to educators and parents: Our editors have carefully reviewed these websites to ensure that they are suitable for students. Many websites change frequently, however, and we cannot guarantee that a site's future contents will continue to meet our high standards of quality and educational value. Be advised that students should be closely supervised whenever they access the Internet.

Index

bolt 12, 21

clamp 14, 21

drill bits 16, 21

drills 16

hold together 4, 10, 12, 14

inclined plane 6

jack 14, 21

jar 20, 21

lid 20

nut 12, 21

ramp 6

screwdriver 8

thread 6, 8, 12, 16, 18

tools 4, 14

turning movement 8, 16, 18

up-and-down movement 8

water 4, 18, 21

wood 4, 8, 14, 16, 21